MILITARY COMMANDO BUG-IN BOOK: The Complete Navy Seals Home Defense Strategy: Transform, Secure and Protection Your Home Against Any Threat.

By

KEVIN N. CLIFTON

Copyright©2024 KEVIN N. CLIFTON

DEDICATION

I dedicate this book to all my wonderful and amazing readers.

This is dedicated to every individual and family who knows that preparation is the foundation of survival. May this guide be a resource to fortify your home, safeguard your loved ones, and empower you to face any challenge with confidence and resilience.

Stay vigilant, stay prepared, and always protect what matters most.

Thank you so much!

TABLE OF CONTENT

INTRODUCTION

Transform Your Home into a Fortress

When danger looms, your home should serve as more than just a place of residence—it must stand as your most formidable line of defense. This Navy SEALs Bug-In Guide equips you with the skills, techniques, and mindset needed to fortify your house and safeguard your loved ones from any threat. Drawing on the proven survival strategies of Navy SEALs, this guide will lead you through the essential steps to convert your home into a well-prepared, secure fortress.

In an unpredictable world, taking proactive measures to prepare for potential disasters is not just wise—it's essential. Whether faced with natural disasters, social unrest, or economic instability, being caught unprepared can lead to dire consequences. This guide aims to change that. By the end of this course, you'll have the knowledge to identify hazards, protect your home, stockpile crucial supplies, and, most importantly, maintain the mental and emotional resilience necessary to navigate any situation.

Why Bug-In?

While many believe that fleeing is the best response during a crisis, bugging out carries its own set of dangers. Roadblocks, hostile environments, scarcity of resources, and general unpredictability can make leaving your home a risky gamble. In contrast, bugging in enables you to remain in a secure and controlled setting, where you've established systems to withstand external challenges.

Navy SEALs are renowned for their ability to thrive in high-pressure situations and operate effectively in dangerous conditions. This guide brings those skills to your doorstep, empowering you to apply military-grade strategies to protect your home and keep your family safe during crises.

The Bug-In Blueprint

This guide outlines the crucial elements of an effective bug-in strategy. You will learn about:

Home Defense: Reinforcing doors, windows, and access points while implementing security measures to deter intruders.

Stockpiling: How to accumulate food, water, medical supplies, and other essentials to sustain you through prolonged crises.

Alternative Power and Communication: Generating power and maintaining communication during grid failures.

Mental Preparedness: Strategies for preserving emotional and psychological strength, ensuring you stay calm and effective under pressure.

Your home is more than just a shelter—it's the foundation of your safety and survival strategy. With the right preparations, you can transform it into a refuge where your family can weather even the toughest challenges. This handbook will instill you with the confidence and skills to achieve that.

So, let's embark on this journey—your home defense mission begins here. By the end, you'll be ready to face any situation that arises, knowing your home is secure and your family is protected.

CHAPTER ONE

Understanding the Bug-In Strategy

Choosing to Stay Put: The Benefits of Bugging In

In times of crisis, one of the most critical decisions you will face is whether to stay at home or evacuate. While many preppers emphasize "bugging out" to seek safer ground, bugging in often proves to be the more advantageous choice. This chapter delves into the bug-in strategy, exploring its definition, when it is most effective, and how to mentally prepare for remaining at home during an emergency.

What Is Bugging In?

Bugging in refers to the practice of staying in your home or a predetermined safe space during an emergency, rather than fleeing. By opting to bug in, you depend on your own resources, supplies, and skills to endure the situation, whether it involves a natural disaster, civil unrest, or another life-threatening event.

The rationale behind bugging in is straightforward: your home is already equipped to meet your basic needs, and leaving can expose you to unnecessary dangers. In a well-prepared home, you have access to food, water, shelter, and security—conditions that may not be guaranteed if you choose to evacuate. Bugging in allows you to maintain control over your environment while avoiding the risks associated with travel, looting, or violence that often accompany mass evacuations.

Key Components of Bugging In

Self-Sufficiency: Bugging in requires you to be fully equipped to meet your family's needs without outside assistance. This includes having ample food, water, medical supplies, and security measures in place.

Safety and Security: Remaining at home enables you to fortify your environment and create a secure sanctuary. You know your neighborhood well and can better manage who has access to your property.

Long-Term Planning: Bugging in isn't just about surviving for a few days; it's about being prepared for extended periods. This necessitates a focus on long-term sustainability, including backup power sources, water purification systems, and strategies for safeguarding your property from various threats.

Why Bugging In May Be Preferable to Bugging Out

Many people believe that during a major crisis, leaving their homes for a remote location is the best choice. However, bugging out can often be riskier than staying put. Here's why:

Familiarity and Control

Your home is your territory—a place you know intimately. You're familiar with its layout, security features, and vulnerabilities, which gives you a significant advantage in defending it. You can easily reinforce windows, doors, and other entry points, and you know where to find your emergency supplies. In contrast, bugging out means navigating the unknown, where unpredictability can lead to situations beyond your control.

Avoiding Chaos on the Road

During a catastrophic event, a mass evacuation can lead to gridlock and dangerous conditions on the roads. Traffic jams, accidents, and even violent encounters can quickly turn your escape plan into a nightmare. Bugging in allows you to sidestep this chaos and stay safely out of harm's way.

Reducing Exposure to Threats

Choosing to evacuate exposes you to multiple dangers— whether encountering desperate individuals, navigating hazardous areas, or facing environmental risks. By staying home, you can minimize these threats. You have shelter from the elements, the ability to remain out of sight, and enhanced protection against opportunistic criminals.

Access to Supplies and Comfort

Leaving home means abandoning the resources you've carefully stockpiled. Even if you have an alternative bug-out location, it's unlikely to be as well-equipped as your own home. Bugging in gives you access to your entire inventory of food, water, medical supplies, tools, and weapons, significantly increasing your chances of survival. Additionally, the familiarity of your home provides comfort, which can be a significant psychological boost during stressful times.

Mobility Considerations

For families with children, elderly members, or individuals with disabilities, bugging out may not be a viable option. Traveling long distances on foot, navigating rough terrain, or spending extended hours in a vehicle can be exhausting and hazardous for those with mobility issues. In many cases, bugging in is not only safer but also more practical.

Historical Context: Successful Bugging In

History offers numerous examples of individuals who opted to shelter in place rather than evacuate, often to their advantage. Here are a few instances where bugging in proved to be the wiser choice:

Hurricanes

During storms, officials frequently advise residents in vulnerable areas to evacuate. However, many inland inhabitants find that staying put is a safer option. For instance, during Hurricane Katrina, many who remained in their well-built homes on higher ground fared better than those who fled into the chaos of overcrowded shelters. Those who bugged in benefited from their stored supplies, shelter from the storm, and the ability to protect their properties, while evacuees often found themselves stranded or in ill-equipped shelters.

World War II Air Raids

During the London Blitz, residents were encouraged to stay put during air raids. Many utilized reinforced areas of their homes or government-provided shelters. By bugging in, they avoided the dangers of rushing through the streets during bombings, allowing them to safeguard their families and homes with minimal losses.

Pandemics and Quarantines

The COVID-19 pandemic highlighted the importance of bugging in. During the outbreak, individuals were urged to remain indoors and limit contact to curb the virus's spread. Those with adequate supplies and a solid bug-in strategy managed to shelter in place, reducing their exposure and waiting for conditions to improve.

Civil Unrest

During periods of civil unrest, staying home can often be the safest option. For example, during the riots following Martin Luther King Jr.'s assassination in 1968, many cities experienced violent protests. Those who secured their homes and chose to remain indoors were able to avoid the chaos and violence in the streets.

Psychological Preparedness: The Role of Mindset in Crisis

While physical preparation is crucial for bugging in, mental and emotional readiness are equally important. A crisis can test your mental limits, and without the right mindset, even the best resources may not be enough. Here are key elements of psychological preparedness:

Acceptance of Reality

The first step in mental preparation is acknowledging the situation. Denial can be dangerous during a crisis.

Some may struggle to accept the severity of the circumstances, leading to poor decision-making or inaction. Acceptance involves recognizing the crisis's seriousness while focusing your thoughts on survival and actionable solutions.

Emotional Control

It's normal to feel overwhelmed during a crisis, especially when fear and uncertainty are at play. Maintaining emotional control is vital for sound decision-making. Techniques such as deep breathing, meditation, or grounding exercises can help manage stress. Allowing panic to take over can lead to reckless choices that jeopardize your safety.

Self-Discipline

Bugging in may require you to ration supplies and adhere to a structured routine. Developing self-discipline is essential for your long-term well-being. Establishing daily routines, setting goals, and maintaining a structured schedule can help you stay organized during chaos. Whether managing food and water or securing your home, discipline will keep you focused.

Mental Flexibility

While having a plan is crucial, no plan is infallible. Crises are unpredictable, and adaptability is key to long-term survival. Mental flexibility means adjusting your strategies based on evolving circumstances, whether that involves modifying your daily routine, finding creative solutions to challenges, or reassessing your overall plan as the situation changes.

Maintaining Morale

Prolonged crises can lead to feelings of anxiety, depression, and despair. It's important to keep morale high, not just for yourself but for your entire household. A positive outlook and a sense of hope, along with fostering connections with loved ones, can significantly boost spirits during tough times. Engage in activities that promote mental well-being, such as reading, playing games, or light exercise. Sharing stories and laughter can strengthen family bonds and enhance overall resilience.

Focusing on the Bigger Picture

In the midst of a crisis, it's easy to become overwhelmed by immediate challenges. However, maintaining perspective is essential. Remind yourself of your long-term goal: survival and recovery. Staying mentally grounded in this purpose will help you persevere through difficult situations and make clear-headed decisions.

The Strength of Bugging In

Bugging in offers clear advantages over bugging out, particularly concerning safety, security, and control over your environment. While bugging out may expose you to numerous dangers and uncertainties, bugging in allows you to rely on the resources you've gathered at home.

However, successful bugging in requires careful preparation, both physically and mentally. In addition to accumulating supplies and securing your home, you must cultivate the right mindset to address the psychological challenges of sheltering in place during a crisis.

Understanding the bug-in strategy, its benefits, and how to prepare physically and emotionally will put you in a stronger position to face any emergency. By staying calm and prepared, you can protect your family and home from whatever challenges lie ahead.

CHAPTER TWO

Assessing Threats to Your Home

When you choose to stay in your home, ensuring its protection becomes your top priority. However, threats to your property can arise from various sources, including natural disasters and human-made crises. To prepare effectively, it's crucial to understand the potential dangers you might face, analyze the specific risks related to your location, and prioritize these threats accordingly. This chapter will guide you in identifying possible hazards to your home and developing a plan to safeguard your loved ones.

Types of Threats

Before you can adequately prepare, it's essential to recognize the various hazards that could impact your property. These threats can be categorized into four main groups: natural disasters, civil unrest, home invasions, and economic collapse. Each category presents unique challenges and requires tailored preparations.

Natural Disasters

Natural disasters are among the most common and potentially destructive threats to your home. They often strike with little warning, leading to significant damage and disruption of essential services. Depending on your geographic location, you may be more susceptible to specific types of disasters. Here are some examples:

Hurricanes: Coastal areas are particularly vulnerable to hurricanes, which bring high winds, storm surges, and flooding that can devastate homes and infrastructure. Inland regions can also experience the aftermath, including heavy rainfall and tornadoes.

Tornadoes: These unpredictable storms can obliterate homes within minutes. If you reside in Tornado Alley or an area prone to these severe weather events, it's vital to protect your property against high winds and debris.

Floods: Flooding is one of the most common natural disasters and can occur virtually anywhere. Whether triggered by heavy rainfall, hurricanes, or dam failures, flooding can cause extensive damage and render roads impassable.

Earthquakes: Living near a fault line poses a serious risk of earthquakes. These seismic events can demolish buildings, disrupt power supplies, and hinder access to emergency services, often without any warning.

Wildfires: In dry, densely forested regions, wildfires can spread rapidly, destroying everything in their path. If you live in a fire-prone area, it's crucial to take proactive measures to protect your home and establish an evacuation plan.

Blizzards and Ice Storms: For those in colder climates, severe winter weather can pose significant threats. Blizzards and ice storms can cause power outages, structural damage, and make travel nearly impossible.

Each natural disaster requires a tailored approach to preparation, making it essential to identify which risks are most significant for your location.

Civil Unrest

Civil unrest encompasses large-scale disturbances resulting from protests, riots, or general societal instability. These events can vary from peaceful demonstrations to violent confrontations, which may include looting and attacks on homes and businesses.

During times of political turmoil, economic hardship, or social tensions, urban areas can become hotspots for civil unrest. If your home is located in or near a densely populated region, the likelihood of riots or looting may increase significantly. Civil unrest can often erupt unexpectedly and spread quickly, leaving you with limited time to respond.

Home Invasions

Home invasions can occur during peaceful times, but their likelihood increases dramatically during crises when law enforcement resources are stretched thin. In such situations, criminals may exploit the chaos, knowing that police response times may be delayed or nonexistent.

During prolonged emergencies—such as economic collapse, civil unrest, or natural disasters—desperation can drive individuals to invade homes in search of food, water, or other vital supplies. To mitigate this threat, it's essential to ensure that your home is secure and well-stocked, making it difficult for intruders to breach your defenses.

Economic Collapse

An economic collapse can result in severe shortages, widespread unemployment, and social chaos. In extreme cases, it may lead to the breakdown of critical services such as healthcare, law enforcement, and utilities. A catastrophic economic downturn could render currency worthless, forcing people to rely on trade and barter for essential goods.

During an economic crisis, crime rates tend to rise as desperation sets in. Incidents of rioting, looting, and home invasions may become more frequent, while access to food and water may dwindle. Preparing for an economic collapse requires a focus on stockpiling supplies, safeguarding your property, and striving for self-sufficiency.

Risk Assessment: Evaluating Specific Risks in Your Area

Recognizing the types of dangers is just the first step; you also need to assess which threats are most likely to affect your property based on your location. Some regions are more susceptible to certain hazards than others. A comprehensive risk assessment involves examining your geographic factors, your home's vulnerabilities, and the socio-political climate in your area.

Geographical Factors

Your location plays a crucial role in determining the types of risks you may encounter. Consider the following:

Coastal Areas: If you live near the coast, your primary threats are likely hurricanes, floods, and storm surges. Depending on your proximity to the water, you may also face risks from rising sea levels or tsunamis.

Mountainous or Forested Regions: In areas surrounded by woods or mountains, your risks may include wildfires, flash floods, and landslides. The dense vegetation and steep terrain can make escape routes more challenging, making bugging in the safer option during a disaster.

Urban Areas: In densely populated cities, threats such as civil unrest, home invasions, and supply shortages are significant concerns. If power infrastructure fails or a prolonged economic collapse occurs, crime rates may escalate. Additionally, evacuating urban areas during a crisis can be difficult due to traffic congestion and roadblocks.

Rural Areas: While rural areas may be less prone to civil unrest, they face their own unique challenges, such as isolation and difficulty accessing emergency services. Natural disasters like wildfires, tornadoes, and winter storms can be particularly dangerous in rural regions, where road conditions may be treacherous.

Vulnerability of Your Home

After analyzing the general hazards in your area, it's important to evaluate your home's specific vulnerabilities. Consider these factors:

Building Materials: Is your home constructed to withstand the most likely hazards in your region? For example, homes in earthquake-prone areas should feature reinforced foundations and flexible materials to absorb shockwaves. In hurricane-prone zones, storm shutters and impact-resistant windows are crucial.

Proximity to Water: If you live near a river, lake, or coastline, flooding should be a primary concern. Even homes situated away from water sources can be at risk of flash floods during heavy rainfall. Elevating your property and keeping sandbags or flood barriers on hand can help minimize flood damage.

Security Features: How well is your home fortified against potential intruders? Strong locks, reinforced doors, security cameras, and motion-sensor lighting are essential for deterring home invasions. If civil unrest or economic collapse is a concern in your area, establishing a secure perimeter and having a defense plan will be vital.

Socio-Political Climate

The socio-political environment of your location can significantly influence the types of risks you face. Consider the following:

Political Instability: Areas experiencing political turmoil—especially during contested elections or widespread protests—are at a higher risk of civil unrest. Stay informed by monitoring local and national news to gauge the level of instability and adjust your preparedness plans accordingly.

Crime Rates: High-crime neighborhoods are more susceptible to home invasions, looting, and theft, particularly during crises. If crime is already a concern in your area, take additional security precautions.

Access to Emergency Services: If you live in a remote location with limited access to police, fire, and medical services, your home may be more vulnerable during a disaster. Without prompt assistance, you will need to be self-sufficient and prepared to manage medical emergencies, fires, and security threats on your own.

Creating a Threat Matrix: Prioritizing Potential Threats

Now that you've identified the potential threats to your home and evaluated the risks in your area, it's time to create a threat matrix. This matrix will help you rank the threats you are most likely to encounter based on two key factors: likelihood and impact. By organizing threats in this manner, you can concentrate your preparations on the most pressing concerns.

Understanding Likelihood vs. Impact

When assessing potential threats, evaluate both the likelihood of each threat occurring and the potential impact it would have on your home and family.

Likelihood: This refers to the probability that a specific threat will occur in your area. For instance, if you live in Florida, the likelihood of a hurricane is high, while the risk of an earthquake is low. Conversely, in California, earthquakes are far more likely, while hurricanes are less of a concern.

Impact: This relates to the severity of damage a threat would cause if it materialized. Even if a threat has a low probability, if its potential consequences are catastrophic, it warrants preparation. For example, while a major earthquake might be unlikely in some areas, the potential destruction it could cause makes it necessary to plan for it.

Assigning Threat Levels

To develop your threat matrix, assign each potential threat a level of likelihood and impact. Here's how to categorize them:

Likelihood:

Low: Unlikely to occur, but possible.

Medium: Possible and should be taken seriously.

High: Likely to happen, based on historical patterns or geographic factors.

Impact:

Low: Minimal harm or disruption; recovery is manageable.

Medium: Significant damage requiring time and resources to remediate.

High: Catastrophic damage that would severely affect your home, safety, and ability to survive.

By assigning these values, you can prioritize your preparedness efforts. For example, if you live in a hurricane-prone area, hurricanes might be classified as a "high-likelihood, high-impact" threat, while tornadoes might be "medium-likelihood, high-impact," depending on your specific location.

Developing a Preparedness Plan

Once you've assessed potential threats and created your threat matrix, the next step is to develop a comprehensive preparedness plan tailored to your unique circumstances. This plan should address each identified threat, outlining specific actions you can take to enhance your home's safety and security.

Emergency Supplies

A well-stocked supply of emergency essentials is vital for surviving various crises. Consider the following items for your emergency kit:

Water: Store at least one gallon of water per person per day for at least three days.

Food: Stockpile non-perishable food items, such as canned goods, dried fruits, nuts, and energy bars.

First Aid Kit: Include bandages, antiseptics, pain relievers, and any necessary prescription medications.

Flashlights and Batteries: Ensure you have reliable light sources in case of power outages.

Multi-tool or Swiss Army Knife: Useful for various tasks during emergencies.

Portable Phone Charger: Keep your devices charged, especially for emergency communication.

Safety and Security Measures

Evaluate your home's security features and make necessary upgrades to fortify your property against potential intrusions or emergencies:

Reinforce Doors and Windows: Install deadbolts, security bars, or shatterproof window film.

Surveillance Systems: Consider investing in security cameras or a home security system for added protection.

Create Safe Zones: Designate specific areas in your home as safe zones, equipped with supplies and communication tools, should a crisis arise.

Emergency Communication Plan

Develop a communication plan for your family and loved ones in case of emergencies. This plan should include:

Meeting Points: Identify safe locations to gather if separated during a crisis.

Emergency Contacts: Compile a list of important contacts, including neighbors, friends, and family members.

Backup Communication Methods: Establish alternative means of communication, such as walkie-talkies or messaging apps that function without Wi-Fi.

3. Example Threat Matrix

Here's an example of how a threat matrix might look for someone living in a coastal city:

Threat	Likelihood	Impact	Priority
Hurricane	High	High	1
Flooding	Medium	High	2

Civil Unrest	Medium	Medium	3
Home Invasion	Medium	High	4
Earthquake	Low	High	5
Wildfire	Low	Medium	6

Based on this matrix, your first priority would be preparing for hurricanes, followed by flooding. Civil unrest and house invasions should be your next concerns, while earthquakes and wildfires—though still possible—are lesser priorities due to their decreased likelihood or impact.

4. Reviewing and Updating Your Threat Matrix

A threat matrix is not a static instrument. As your circumstances change—whether by relocation to a new area, alterations in the socio-political climate, or changes in weather patterns—you'll need to assess and update your matrix. For example, if you see an upsurge in civil unrest in your area, you may need to boost its priority level and alter your preparations accordingly.

Additionally, as you perform certain preparation activities, you can lessen the impact level of particular dangers. For instance, if you've reinforced your home against hurricanes, the potential impact of a hurricane might reduce from "high" to "medium," allowing you to focus on other worries.

Proactive Assessment Is the Key to Survival

Assessing the threats to your house is the core of your bug-in strategy. By knowing the types of dangers you encounter, evaluating the hazards particular to your location, and building a prioritized plan through a threat matrix, you can make informed decisions about how to best safeguard your home and your loved ones. It's better to plan now, when you have the time and resources, than to be caught off guard in the midst of a crisis. With a clear sense of what you're up against, you may take actions to defend your property and your peace of mind.

CHAPTER THREE

Fortifying Your Home

The Importance of Physical Security in Your Home

Physical security is crucial for safeguarding your home. Your home is your sanctuary, and ensuring it remains a safe and secure environment for you and your loved ones is paramount. Whether faced with civil disturbances, break-ins, or potential natural disasters, bolstering your home's defenses will help you rest easier at night and provide peace of mind. In this chapter, we will explore practical steps you can take to enhance your home security, from strengthening windows and doors to creating safe spaces for emergencies.

Fortifying Windows and Doors: Your First Line of Defense

Windows and doors serve as the most visible entry points to your home, making them the most vulnerable to breaches. Strengthening these areas should be your top priority.

Reinforcing Exterior Doors

Your exterior doors are your primary defense against outside threats. If they are weak or easily accessible, all your other security efforts could be undermined. Here are ways to reinforce them:

Install Solid-Core Doors: Many homes come with hollow-core doors, which are lightweight and inexpensive but offer little protection. Opt for solid-core doors made of wood, steel, or fiberglass for superior resistance to forced entry. If your current doors lack strength, consider replacing them as a priority.

Use Long Screws for Door Hinges: The screws that secure your door hinges are vital to their strength. Replace standard ¾-inch screws with longer screws (at least 3 inches) to better anchor the door to the frame. This simple adjustment makes it significantly harder for someone to kick the door open.

Add a Deadbolt Lock: If your exterior doors lack deadbolts, installing one is essential. Choose a lock with a one-inch throw bolt and ensure it's installed securely. Don't forget to reinforce the strike plate (the metal plate where the bolt meets the door frame) with long screws as well.

Incorporate a Door Barricade or Reinforcement Plate: For additional protection, consider installing a door barricade, which locks in place to prevent forced entry, or a reinforcement plate that adds metal protection around the lock and strike plate.

Securing Sliding Glass Doors

Sliding glass doors are another common weak point in home security. If not properly secured, they can be easily compromised. Here are some measures to enhance their security:

Install a Sliding Door Security Bar: This bar fits along the bottom track of the sliding door, preventing it from being opened, even if the lock is picked or broken. It's an affordable yet effective deterrent.

Add a Locking Pin: A locking pin can be used to physically secure the door to the frame, making it nearly impossible for someone to lift or force it open.

Apply Shatterproof Film: Since sliding glass doors are made of glass, applying shatterproof film can help prevent shattering if someone attempts to break in, complicating an intruder's efforts to gain entry.

Reinforcing Windows

Windows also present vulnerable access points. Here's how to protect them effectively:

Install Window Locks: Many windows come equipped with basic latches that can be easily forced open. Upgrade to sturdier locks to deter break-ins. Consider installing keyed locks that require a key to open from the inside.

Use Window Bars or Grilles: If you live in a high-crime area, adding window bars or grilles can provide extra protection. While they may not be the most aesthetically pleasing option, they are highly effective in keeping intruders out.

Apply Security Film: Similar to sliding doors, applying security film to your windows can prevent glass from shattering if someone tries to break in, reinforcing the glass and making it tougher to breach.

Install Window Sensors: Many modern home security systems include window sensors that alert you if a window is opened or broken, allowing you to stay informed of any potential intrusions.

Installing Security Systems: A Deterrent and Detection Mechanism

A home security system can be an invaluable tool for securing your property. Not only does it deter potential burglars, but it also provides notifications and real-time updates in the event of a break-in. With various types of systems available, it's essential to choose one that fits your needs and budget.

Security Cameras

Security cameras are among the most effective ways to monitor your home and deter criminal activity. Here's how to maximize your camera system:

Position Cameras at Key Entry Points: Ensure cameras are placed at all major entry points, such as front and back doors, garage doors, and any side entrances. The cameras should be positioned to capture clear footage of anyone approaching.

Utilize Motion-Activated Cameras: Motion-activated cameras begin recording only when they detect movement, which saves you the hassle of sifting through hours of footage. Many systems can send alerts to your phone when motion is detected, enabling real-time monitoring.

Install Cameras Inside Your Home: In addition to exterior cameras, consider placing cameras inside your home, particularly in high-traffic areas like hallways or stairwells. This can help identify intruders if they manage to enter.

Alarm Systems

An alarm system adds another critical layer of security. It not only alerts you to a break-in but also has the potential to scare off intruders before they can steal anything. Look for the following features in an alarm system:

24/7 Monitoring: Some alarm systems connect to a monitoring service that notifies authorities if the alarm is triggered, providing peace of mind, especially when you're away from home.

Door and Window Sensors: Most alarm systems include sensors that can be installed on doors and windows to detect when they are opened, triggering the alarm if someone attempts entry.

Glass Break Detectors: These sensors are designed to detect the sound of breaking glass, making them particularly useful for safeguarding windows and sliding doors.

Panic Buttons: Many modern alarm systems feature panic buttons that can be pressed in emergencies, immediately triggering the alarm and alerting the monitoring service.

Motion Sensors and Lighting

Motion sensors can detect movement both inside and outside your home. When combined with exterior lighting, they serve as an excellent deterrent:

Install Motion-Sensing Lights: These lights activate upon detecting movement, illuminating dark areas around your property. This can deter potential burglars and alert you to their presence.

Place Motion Sensors in Key Areas: Inside your home, install motion sensors in hallways, stairwells, or other areas likely to be traversed by an intruder. These sensors can activate an alert if movement is detected while the system is armed.

Defensive Landscaping: Natural Barriers for Security

While reinforcing physical security measures is vital, defensive landscaping can provide an additional layer of protection. Strategic landscaping can hinder burglars from approaching your home unnoticed or accessing vulnerable entry points.

Planting Thorny Shrubs and Bushes

One of the simplest and most effective ways to deter burglars is by planting thorny plants near windows and other entry points. These natural barriers can make it difficult and uncomfortable for someone attempting to break in.

Consider Plants like Rose Bushes, Holly, and Pyracantha: These plants are excellent natural deterrents due to their sharp thorns, making it painful for someone to climb through a window or break in.

Strategic Placement: Ensure these bushes are close enough to your windows to offer protection but not so close that they provide cover for intruders. Maintain a clear view of your windows from the street to discourage would-be thieves.

Creating Barriers with Fencing and Gates

Fencing is another crucial element of defensive landscaping. A robust fence can significantly hinder an intruder's ability to access your property:

Install a Tall, Sturdy Fence: A tall fence serves as a physical barrier to keep intruders at bay. Opt for a design that is difficult to climb, such as one with pointed tops or a privacy fence that lacks handholds.

Add a Locking Gate: Ensure any gates leading to your yard or driveway are robust and equipped with secure locks. A locked gate adds another obstacle for intruders, increasing the likelihood that they'll abandon their attempt.

Use Gravel Paths: Gravel paths are noisy to walk on, making it difficult for someone to approach your property without being heard. Consider using gravel around key areas, such as near windows or the perimeter of your yard.

Lighting and Visibility

Proper lighting is a critical component of any security strategy. Intruders are less likely to target a well-lit home, as they prefer to remain hidden. Here's how to leverage lighting to your advantage:

Install Outdoor Lighting: Bright lights surrounding the exterior of your home make it challenging for anyone to approach unnoticed. Focus on entry points like doors and windows, as well as areas where someone could hide.

Utilize Motion-Sensing Lights: These lights only activate when someone is nearby, which can surprise intruders and alert you to their presence without the need for constant illumination.

Trim Trees and Bushes: Overgrown vegetation can provide cover for intruders. Regularly maintain your landscaping to eliminate hiding spots and ensure clear visibility of your property from the street.

Creating Safe Rooms: A Secure Retreat in Emergencies

Even with robust home defenses, situations may arise when you need to retreat to a designated safe area. Whether faced with a home invasion, natural disaster, or civil unrest, having a safe room provides a secure space until help arrives.

Choosing a Location for Your Safe Room

When selecting the location of your safe room, consider factors such as accessibility, structural integrity, and proximity to exits. Ideally, your safe room should be easy to access in an emergency yet difficult for intruders to reach:

Select Interior Rooms: An interior room with no windows is often the best option for a safe room. Consider spaces like a basement, pantry, or closet.

Ensure Reinforced Walls: The room's walls should be sturdy enough to withstand potential breaches. Consider reinforcing them with plywood or other materials if necessary.

Add an External Door: If possible, install a secure door that can be locked from the inside, providing an extra layer of protection.

Equipping Your Safe Room

A well-equipped safe room can significantly enhance your safety in emergencies. Here are essential items to include:

Communication Devices: Ensure your safe room has a landline or mobile phone with sufficient battery backup to call for help.

Basic Supplies: Keep a supply of water, non-perishable food, first-aid kits, flashlights, and batteries to sustain you during an emergency.

Emergency Plan: Create a family emergency plan outlining how to access the safe room and what to do in case of an emergency.

Safety Features: Consider adding a camera to monitor the area outside the safe room and a way to barricade the door from the inside.

Your Home, Your Sanctuary

Your home should be a place of comfort and security. By investing time and resources into enhancing your physical security, you protect not only your property but also your peace of mind. From reinforcing windows and doors to installing security systems and creating safe spaces, every step you take to secure your home is a step towards ensuring your family's safety.

In the following chapters, we will explore additional strategies for security, including digital safety, emergency preparedness, and developing a community security network. Each facet of security is interconnected, working together to create a holistic safety plan that allows you to thrive in your home without fear.

CHAPTER FOUR

Stockpiling Essential Supplies

Preparing for Uncertainty: The Necessity of Stockpiling Essential Supplies

In unpredictable times, preparedness shifts from being a mere suggestion to an essential requirement. Stockpiling basic supplies such as food, water, and medical essentials can provide a sense of security and peace of mind when unforeseen circumstances arise. Whether you're preparing for natural disasters, economic challenges, or emergencies, having these supplies readily available can significantly impact your ability to cope. This chapter offers practical, step-by-step guidance on how to build a robust stockpile that ensures your family's safety and well-being.

Food Storage: Creating a Sustainable Food Stockpile

Building a food stockpile goes beyond simply grabbing items off the shelf; it requires careful planning to ensure the food you store remains nutritious and easy to prepare over time. Follow these guidelines to create a stockpile that can sustain you for weeks, months, or even longer if necessary.

Prioritize Shelf Life

The shelf life of the food you store is paramount. Choose items that can last without losing their nutritional value or becoming unsafe to eat. Avoid foods with high moisture content or those that are perishable. Here are some long-lasting food options to consider:

Canned Goods: Properly preserved vegetables, beans, meats, and soups can last for years. Opt for low-sodium and low-fat varieties when possible.

Dried Foods: Items like pasta, rice, oats, and beans, when stored in sealed containers, can remain edible for a long time.

Freeze-Dried Foods: Lightweight and easy to store, freeze-dried fruits, vegetables, and meals can last for decades.

Grains: Wheat, quinoa, barley, and similar grains have extended shelf lives and can be used in various recipes.

Honey: This natural sweetener never spoils and can serve as a cooking ingredient or sugar substitute.

Peanut Butter: High in protein and calories, peanut butter can last for years without refrigeration.

Rotate Your Stockpile

Regularly rotating your stockpile is crucial to ensure the food remains fresh. Follow the "first in, first out" principle: when you purchase fresh food, place it behind the older items. This practice minimizes waste and prevents expired food from going to waste.

Diversify Your Food Supply

Avoid relying on a single type of food for your stockpile. While staples like rice and beans are great, they lack the variety needed for a balanced diet. Include a range of foods from different dietary groups:

Proteins: Canned meats, beans, lentils, and nut butters.

Carbohydrates: Rice, pasta, crackers, and oats.

Fruits and Vegetables: Canned or freeze-dried options.

Dairy: Powdered milk or long-lasting cheeses like aged cheddar.

Fats: Olive oil, coconut oil, or shelf-stable butter.

By diversifying your stock, you ensure a balanced diet and avoid food fatigue, which can be detrimental to healthy eating during stressful times.

Consider Special Dietary Needs

When stockpiling food, consider any dietary restrictions or unique needs within your family. Whether it's allergies, lactose intolerance, or specific nutritional requirements, ensure your stockpile accommodates everyone. While it may require extra effort, providing options for gluten-free grains or plant-based proteins is essential.

Store Food Properly

Proper storage is vital for maximizing the longevity of your stockpile. Keep your food in a cool, dry place free from pests. Basements, pantries, and dedicated storage areas work well. Avoid humid or extreme temperature areas like garages or attics. Use sealed containers to protect against spoilage and pests. For grains or flours, consider oxygen absorbers or vacuum-sealed containers to enhance shelf life.

Cooking and Preparation

In emergencies, you may lack access to your regular cooking equipment. Include items in your stockpile that require minimal preparation or can be eaten without cooking. Options like instant meals, canned goods, and ready-to-eat snacks are valuable. Remember to pack manual can openers, portable burners, or other cooking tools that don't depend on electricity.

Water Reserves: Storage and Purification Methods

While you can survive for weeks without food, going without water for just a few days can be life-threatening. Ensuring you have an adequate supply of clean water is essential for any emergency plan. Here's how to guarantee you have enough water and ensure its safety for drinking.

Determine Water Storage Needs

A general guideline is to store at least one gallon of water per person each day. This amount covers drinking, cooking, and hygiene. For a family of four, that means a minimum of 12 gallons for three days. However, for extended emergencies, aim for at least two weeks' worth of water for each person.

Proper Water Storage

Use clean, food-grade containers specifically designed for long-term water storage. Consider these options:

Commercial Bottled Water: Convenient but often suitable for short-term use; remember to rotate them frequently.

Water Storage Containers: Large, food-grade plastic containers or water barrels (55-gallon drums) are ideal for long-term storage.

Collapsible Water Containers: Useful for short-term storage or for filling during an impending disaster.

Store water in a cool, dark location away from direct sunlight, and label containers with storage dates, changing the water every six months.

Purifying Water

If your stored water becomes contaminated or runs out, have a plan for purifying water from other sources, such as rain, rivers, or lakes. Reliable methods include:

Boiling: The most effective way to kill bacteria, viruses, and parasites. Bring water to a rolling boil for at least one minute.

Water Purification Tablets: Small and easy to store, these tablets chemically treat water to make it safe to drink.

Water Filters: Portable filters, such as pump-style or straw filters, remove contaminants from water.

Bleach: In an emergency, add 1/8 teaspoon (8 drops) of unscented bleach per gallon of water, stir, and let it sit for 30 minutes before drinking.

Rainwater Collection

For long-term water supply concerns, consider implementing a rainwater collection system. With the right setup, you can harvest rainwater from your roof and store it for later use. Ensure your system includes filters to eliminate debris and impurities before storage. Remember that rainwater may still require purification before consumption, especially if collected from a rooftop.

Medical Supplies: Essential First Aid Kits and Medications

In emergencies, medical supplies can be just as critical as food and water. Injuries, illnesses, or chronic conditions can escalate into life-threatening situations without the appropriate resources. A well-stocked first aid kit and essential medications are fundamental components of your emergency preparedness plan.

First Aid Kit Essentials

Customize your first aid kit to your family's specific needs, but certain items should be included in every kit. Essential supplies for treating common injuries and illnesses include:

Bandages: A variety of adhesive bandages, sterile gauze pads, and adhesive tape for larger wounds.

Antiseptics: Antiseptic wipes or solutions, like hydrogen peroxide or rubbing alcohol, to clean wounds and prevent infection.

Antibiotic Ointment: Useful for cuts, scrapes, and burns to promote healing and prevent infection.

Pain Relievers: Over-the-counter medications like ibuprofen, acetaminophen, or aspirin for pain relief and fever reduction.

Tweezers and Scissors: Handy for removing splinters or cutting tape and bandages.

Thermometer: Essential for monitoring fevers, a key sign of infection or illness.

Instant Cold Packs: Effective for reducing swelling and pain from injuries like sprains or fractures.

Elastic Bandages: For wrapping sprains or supporting injured joints.

Gloves: Disposable gloves to protect yourself when treating wounds or handling medical supplies.

First Aid Manual: A reliable first aid book can guide you in treating medical emergencies when professional help isn't accessible.

Medications to Stockpile

In addition to first aid supplies, maintaining a supply of medications is crucial, especially for household members with chronic conditions. Consider the following:

Prescription Medications: Whenever possible, keep at least a 30-day supply of essential prescriptions. Consult your doctor about obtaining an emergency supply.

Over-the-Counter Medications: Stock pain relievers, antihistamines (for allergies), antacids, and anti-diarrheal medications for common ailments.

Vitamins and Supplements: In extended emergencies, you might not receive all necessary nutrients from your diet alone; a multivitamin can help fill any gaps.

Inhalers and Epinephrine: Ensure you have extra inhalers and EpiPens for household members with asthma or severe allergies.

Special Medical Needs

For those with unique medical requirements, such as insulin for diabetes or a nebulizer for respiratory issues, have a plan in place to maintain an adequate supply. For example, consider how to keep insulin cool during a power outage or provide battery backups for medical devices.

Sanitation and Hygiene Supplies

Good hygiene is critical during emergencies to prevent illness. In addition to medical supplies, stock up on the following hygiene essentials:

Hand Sanitizer: A valuable alternative when water is scarce, helping to keep hands clean and reduce the spread of germs.

Soap and Disinfectants: Essential for cleaning surfaces and maintaining a sanitary living environment.

Toilet Paper and Sanitary Wipes: Ensure you have enough toilet paper, tissues, and wipes for personal hygiene needs.

Face Masks and Gloves: Crucial for preventing the spread of illness, especially during pandemics or outbreaks.

Empowering Yourself for Uncertain Times

The foundation of preparedness lies in understanding the specific needs of your family and acting accordingly. Stockpiling essential supplies—food, water, and medical items—can help you navigate unpredictable situations and ensure your family's health and safety. By adopting a proactive approach and implementing the strategies outlined in this chapter, you are not only preparing for emergencies but also empowering yourself to face the uncertainties that lie ahead.

Remember, the goal of stockpiling is to reduce anxiety and increase confidence in your ability to handle whatever challenges may arise. Start small, gradually build your stockpile, and involve your family in the process to foster a sense of preparedness and security that extends beyond material supplies.

CHAPTER FIVE

Power and Communication Strategies

When disasters strike, access to reliable electricity and communication becomes crucial. Without them, staying informed, keeping essential devices running, and maintaining contact with loved ones can become incredibly difficult. In this chapter, we'll explore how to generate your own electricity using solar power or backup generators, establish a solid emergency communication plan, and stay informed during crises through radios and other technologies.

Alternative Energy Sources: Generating Your Own Power

When the power grid goes down, having the ability to generate your own electricity becomes essential. Whether it's keeping food fresh, powering medical devices, or maintaining communication, backup power gives you control over the situation. We'll cover two main options: solar power systems and backup generators.

Solar Power: A Sustainable Energy Source

Solar energy is one of the most dependable and eco-friendly ways to generate electricity in an emergency. With the right equipment, you can harness sunlight during the day and store the energy in batteries for later use. This method frees you from relying on traditional fuel sources like gasoline or propane, which may be scarce in a prolonged crisis.

Key Components of a Solar Power System:

Solar Panels: These capture sunlight and convert it into electricity. The number of panels you need depends on your energy requirements and the amount of sun in your area.

Battery Storage: Batteries store excess energy generated during the day for use at night or during cloudy weather.

Inverter: Converts the direct current (DC) produced by solar panels into alternating current (AC) for household use.

Charge Controller: Ensures batteries are charged safely and prevents overcharging.

While solar power systems require a significant initial investment, they offer long-term security and independence. Once set up, they are low-maintenance and produce clean energy without relying on fossil fuels or vulnerable supply chains.

Benefits of Solar Power in Emergencies:

No Fuel Required: As long as the sun shines, you'll have power without needing to store fuel.

Quiet Operation: Solar systems are silent, unlike generators, which can be important for safety in certain emergencies.

Long-Term Solution: Solar panels can last over 25 years, making them a reliable option.

Limitations:

Upfront Costs: The initial investment, especially with battery storage, can be high.

Weather Dependent: Solar generation is reduced during cloudy days or storms.

Limited Output: Depending on your system's size, it may not power everything in your home.

Backup Generators: On-Demand Power

For a more immediate or budget-friendly solution, backup generators are a popular choice. These devices generate power on demand by burning gasoline, propane, or diesel, providing a quick and reliable source of electricity during unexpected outages.

Types of Backup Generators:

Portable Generators: These are compact, affordable, and easy to transport. Ideal for powering a few essential appliances, they require manual operation and frequent refueling.

Standby Generators: Permanently installed outside your home, these automatically turn on during outages and can power your entire house. They often run on natural gas or propane and are suitable for powering major appliances and medical equipment.

Considerations for Generators:

Fuel Supply: Ensure you have enough fuel stored to last through an extended outage. Gasoline has a shorter shelf life, while propane and diesel can be stored longer.

Maintenance: Generators require regular upkeep, including oil changes and inspections, to ensure they function properly when needed.

Noise: Generators can be noisy, which may attract unwanted attention during emergencies. Factor this into your security planning.

Choosing Between Solar Power and Generators

The choice between solar and generators depends on your priorities. If you want a sustainable, long-term solution that doesn't rely on fuel, solar is ideal. If you need an immediate, high-power option, a generator might be more suitable.

Combining Solar and Generators

For maximum preparedness, many people combine solar and generator systems. Solar power can handle daily energy needs, while a generator provides backup when solar isn't sufficient. This hybrid approach ensures you're covered in both short- and long-term grid failures.

Emergency Communication Plans: Staying Connected in a Crisis

The ability to communicate during an emergency is critical. Whether you need to check on family, call for help, or stay informed, a well-thought-out communication plan is essential.

Step 1: Choosing a Primary Communication Method

Decide on a primary form of communication for your household or group. While cell phones are the most common, plan for situations where the network may be down.

Options for Emergency Communication:

Cell Phones: Keep phones charged and consider portable battery packs or solar chargers. Use text messages to conserve battery and avoid network congestion.

Landlines: If you have a landline, it can serve as a backup if phone lines remain functional.

Walkie-Talkies: For short-range communication, walkie-talkies are reliable when cell service is unavailable. Test them beforehand to ensure everyone knows how to use them.

Satellite Phones: These offer a dependable communication line anywhere in the world, though they can be costly.

Step 2: Establishing Meeting Points and Contacts

Set up a meeting point in case communication fails, and designate an out-of-town contact to relay messages between family members if local lines are overwhelmed.

Step 3: Practice and Update the Plan

Make sure everyone in your group understands and practices the plan regularly. Update it as your household or circumstances change.

Step 4: Backup Power for Communication Devices

Ensure you have backup power for communication tools. Portable battery packs, solar chargers, and car chargers can keep your devices powered. A small generator dedicated to communication devices is also a good idea.

Staying Informed: Tools for Real-Time Updates

Access to real-time information during emergencies is critical for making informed decisions. Whether it's evacuation orders, weather updates, or essential service information, the right tools can keep you connected.

Radios: Reliable Information Sources

Battery-operated or hand-crank radios are a dependable way to stay informed when the power is out, and cell networks are down.

Types of Radios:

AM/FM Radios: Tune in to local stations for news and updates.

Weather Radios: NOAA weather radios provide alerts and information specific to weather emergencies and can run on batteries, solar, or hand cranks.

Shortwave Radios: These can pick up transmissions from around the world, offering a broader range of information.

Mobile Apps and Alerts

If your phone is working, apps from organizations like the Red Cross and FEMA can send real-time emergency alerts. These notifications often provide crucial details, such as when and where to evacuate.

Scanners and Emergency Feeds

Police scanners and apps that provide emergency service feeds allow you to stay updated on unfolding local events.

Social Media and News Websites

Platforms like Twitter and Facebook, along with news websites, often offer real-time updates during disasters.

Ensuring Power and Communication Readiness

Preparing for disasters requires careful planning for both power generation and communication. By investing in alternative energy sources like solar panels or generators, and establishing a clear communication strategy, you can stay connected and informed during emergencies. Preparing ahead not only involves gathering the right tools but also knowing how to use them effectively when it matters most.

CHAPTER SIX

Self-Defense Tactics

When emergencies strike, protecting yourself and your family becomes a top priority. While no one wishes to face such situations, being prepared is essential. This chapter covers three critical aspects of personal safety during uncertain times: basic self-defense techniques, situational awareness, and creating a family defense plan.

Basic Self-Defense Techniques: Protecting Yourself and Your Family

Self-defense goes beyond just knowing how to throw a punch or use a weapon. It's about de-escalating situations, avoiding unnecessary conflict, and protecting yourself when danger is unavoidable. In a crisis, quick, effective actions are crucial since there may be no time for hesitation.

The Importance of Simple, Effective Moves

Under stress, the brain often enters a fight-or-flight mode, making complex techniques difficult to recall. The focus should be on learning simple moves that are easy to execute and can incapacitate an attacker long enough for you to escape or get help.

Key Areas to Target

Certain areas on an attacker's body are particularly vulnerable. Targeting these spots can quickly neutralize a threat:

Eyes: A strike to the eyes can temporarily blind the aggressor, allowing you to escape.

Throat: A strong hit to the throat can impede breathing.

Groin: This area is highly sensitive in men and can incapacitate with minimal force.

Knees: Kicking the knees can cause the attacker to lose balance or fall.

Practical Self-Defense Moves

Palm Strike to the Nose: Use the heel of your palm to thrust upward into the attacker's nose. It's a simple but effective disorienting move.

Elbow Strike: In close range, an elbow strike to the face, chest, or ribs can cause significant damage.

Knee to the Groin: If the attacker is too close for punches, a knee to the groin can incapacitate them quickly.

Escape from a Wrist Grab: If your wrist is grabbed, twist your hand toward the attacker's thumb—the weakest point in their grip.

Kick to the Kneecap: A strong kick to the front of the knee can buckle an attacker's leg, making it hard for them to continue the assault.

Defensive Posture

If you sense an impending confrontation, assume a defensive stance. Stand with your feet shoulder-width apart, one foot slightly ahead of the other, and hands up with palms facing outward. This position prepares you to defend without appearing aggressive, potentially helping to de-escalate the situation.

When to Use Self-Defense

Self-defense should always be a last resort. If you can avoid conflict by escaping or defusing the situation, that's ideal. However, if you or your family face physical threats, it's vital to act decisively. Strike with enough force to neutralize the attacker and then escape as quickly as possible.

Situational Awareness: Recognizing and Responding to Potential Threats

The best way to stay safe is to avoid danger in the first place. Situational awareness involves being alert to your surroundings and recognizing potential threats before they escalate. This isn't about being paranoid but rather about staying prepared and vigilant.

The Basics of Situational Awareness

Situational awareness is about understanding what's happening around you and anticipating problems before they arise. It's a proactive rather than reactive approach to personal safety.

Color Codes of Awareness

The Cooper Color Code system is widely used in self-defense to describe levels of situational awareness:

White (Unaware): You're not paying attention, making you vulnerable.

Yellow (Relaxed Awareness): You're calm but alert to your surroundings, noting potential dangers and exits.

Orange (Focused Awareness): You've identified a potential threat and are weighing your options.

Red (Action): The threat is imminent, and you must act, whether by defending yourself or fleeing.

Staying in the "yellow" state—relaxed but aware—allows you to recognize and avoid threats before they become dangerous.

How to Develop Situational Awareness

Scan Your Environment: Regularly assess who's around you and identify potential escape routes.

Trust Your Instincts: If something feels off, trust your gut. Your subconscious may pick up on subtle signs of danger before your conscious mind does.

Avoid Distractions: In vulnerable situations, like walking alone, stay off your phone and be mindful of your surroundings.

Stick to Well-Lit, Public Areas: Whenever possible, avoid isolated areas, especially at night. Criminals are less likely to target you in visible, crowded spaces.

Recognize Dangerous Situations: If you observe someone acting aggressively or following you, don't hesitate to leave. It's better to be cautious than risk harm.

Responding to Threats

If you identify a potential threat, leave the area if possible. Don't wait for the situation to escalate. If escape isn't an option, prepare to defend yourself by assuming a defensive posture or arming yourself with a self-defense tool.

Family Defense Plans: Coordinating a Response with Loved Ones

Being prepared as a family can provide peace of mind during a crisis. Developing a family defense plan ensures everyone knows what to do in an emergency and how to work together to stay safe.

Step 1: Identify Potential Threats

Start by identifying the threats most likely to affect your family, whether natural disasters, civil unrest, or home invasions. Tailor your defense plan to address these specific risks.

Step 2: Designate Roles and Responsibilities

In an emergency, every family member should know their role. For example, who will call for help, and who will secure the children? Assign tasks to each family member:

Adults: One may secure the home, while the other gathers the children.

Children: Teach younger children to go to a safe room and older children to call for help or use basic self-defense tools.

Step 3: Safe Rooms and Escape Routes

Designate a safe room in your home with a strong door, a deadbolt, and essential supplies like water, first aid, and a communication device. Also, establish escape routes and meeting places outside the home in case fleeing is necessary.

Step 4: Self-Defense Tools and Training

If comfortable, consider equipping your family with self-defense tools such as pepper spray, tasers, or firearms (if legal in your area). Ensure that everyone is trained and comfortable using these tools safely.

Step 5: Conduct Drills

Regular practice is key to a successful family defense plan. Conduct drills for different scenarios, like home invasions or natural disasters, at different times of day. The more familiar everyone is with the plan, the more confident they'll be in an emergency.

Step 6: Communication During Emergencies

Ensure every family member knows how to contact emergency services and when to do so. Backup communication devices, such as walkie-talkies, can be useful if cell service fails during a disaster.

By mastering basic self-defense techniques, staying alert through situational awareness, and having a coordinated family plan, you can navigate dangerous situations with greater confidence and security. Preparedness can make all the difference in keeping you and your loved ones safe when facing unforeseen threats.

CHAPTER SEVEN

Mental Resilience and Preparation

When crises hit, your greatest asset is your intellect. While physical preparation is essential, mental resilience is key to ensuring that even the best-laid plans don't fall apart under pressure. In this chapter, we'll explore how to cultivate emotional strength, manage stress and fear, and leverage the support of your community. Each of these elements is vital to maintaining your mental health and equipping you to face any challenges life presents.

Building Emotional Strength: Staying Calm in Crisis

Crises can strike unexpectedly—whether it's a natural disaster, economic turmoil, or a personal emergency. While you can't control everything around you, you can train your mind to stay calm and respond effectively. Emotional strength isn't about suppressing feelings but learning to manage them with clarity and control.

Why Emotional Strength Matters

Emotional strength enables you to keep a clear head when everything around you seems chaotic. During high-stress situations, emotions like fear, anger, or panic can cloud your judgment, leading to poor decisions. The more emotionally resilient you are, the better equipped you'll be to assess the situation, think critically, and act wisely. People who remain emotionally grounded during a crisis often emerge stronger and better prepared for future challenges.

Techniques for Building Emotional Strength

Emotional strength develops over time through consistent effort. The following methods will help you stay mentally grounded and ready to face challenges as they arise.

Mindfulness and Meditation

Mindfulness is the practice of staying present and aware without judgment. During a crisis, it's easy to get swept up in fear of the unknown or regret about what could have been done differently. Mindfulness keeps you focused on the present moment, enabling you to respond thoughtfully rather than react impulsively.

To cultivate mindfulness:

Start with simple breathing exercises, focusing on your breath to anchor yourself in the present.

Set aside a few minutes each day for meditation to help train your mind to stay calm under stress.

Practice observing your thoughts without attaching emotions to them, which can lead to clearer decision-making in high-pressure situations.

Controlled Breathing

When anxiety starts to take over, your body triggers its fight-or-flight response—your heart rate spikes, your muscles tense, and your breathing becomes shallow. This response can amplify fear, creating a vicious cycle. Controlled breathing can break this cycle by calming your nervous system.

A simple exercise:

Inhale through your nose for a count of four.

Hold your breath for four counts.

Slowly exhale through your mouth for four counts.

Repeat this process until you feel your mind and body relax.

Practicing controlled breathing regularly allows you to use this technique whenever you feel anxiety creeping in.

Cognitive Reframing

Your thoughts have a powerful influence on your emotions. Cognitive reframing helps you shift negative or distorted thoughts into more positive, constructive ones. Instead of allowing a crisis to overwhelm you with fear, cognitive reframing encourages you to view the situation from a new perspective.

For example:

Instead of thinking, "I can't handle this," reframe it as: "This is hard, but I've overcome challenges before, and I can do it again."

Instead of focusing on what might go wrong, ask yourself, "What's within my control?" and "What's the next small step I can take?"

By shifting your focus to what you can control, you reduce feelings of helplessness and regain a sense of empowerment, even in difficult situations.

Developing a Growth Mindset

A growth mindset views challenges and setbacks as opportunities for learning and growth. By seeing difficult experiences as chances to build resilience, you change your relationship with hardship. Rather than feeling defeated, you recognize that every crisis is an opportunity to strengthen your emotional resolve.

To foster a growth mindset:

Embrace adversity as part of life, not just as setbacks.

Reflect on past challenges to see how you've grown or what you've learned.

Encourage yourself with positive self-talk, reminding yourself that you are capable of overcoming obstacles.

Stress Management: Coping with Anxiety and Fear

In a crisis, stress and anxiety are inevitable. While you can't eliminate stress entirely, you can manage it to minimize its impact on your mental and physical health. Left unchecked, chronic stress can lead to burnout and emotional exhaustion. However, with the right strategies, you can maintain your resilience and keep performing well, even under pressure.

Recognizing Stress Signs

The first step in managing stress is recognizing its signs. Stress manifests in different ways, and identifying these signals helps you take action before it becomes overwhelming. Common signs of stress include:

Irritability or mood swings

Difficulty concentrating

Trouble sleeping or insomnia

Increased heart rate or muscle tension

Fatigue or low energy

Feeling anxious, overwhelmed, or out of control

When you notice these signs, it's important to take steps to lower your stress levels.

Strategies for Managing Stress

There's no one-size-fits-all solution for stress, but several strategies can help. The key is finding what works best for you and incorporating it into your routine.

Physical Exercise

Exercise is one of the most effective ways to manage stress. Moving your body releases endorphins—natural chemicals that boost your mood and reduce anxiety.

Regular exercise also promotes better sleep, which is essential for mental well-being.

Even if you're not a fitness enthusiast, simple activities like walking, stretching, or doing bodyweight exercises can make a big difference. The goal is to move your body and clear your mind.

Journaling

Writing down your thoughts and emotions can be a powerful tool for relieving stress. Journaling helps you process what's going on internally and provides a space to release pent-up feelings. It also allows you to organize your thoughts and gain clarity on the challenges you're facing.

If you're feeling anxious or stressed, set aside a few minutes daily to write about what's on your mind. Focus on what's causing your stress, how it's affecting you, and any actions you can take to alleviate it. Sometimes, simply putting your thoughts on paper can provide relief.

Progressive Muscle Relaxation

Progressive muscle relaxation (PMR) is a technique that involves tensing and then relaxing different muscle groups in your body. This technique helps release physical tension that often accompanies stress and anxiety. By learning to recognize where your body holds tension, you can consciously relax those areas.

Here's how to practice PMR:

Start at your feet and work your way up your body, tensing each muscle group for five seconds before releasing.

Focus on your calves, thighs, stomach, chest, arms, shoulders, and face.

As you release the tension, take slow, deep breaths to help your body relax fully.

Regular practice of PMR can help you identify and release stress-related tension more quickly.

Time Management and Setting Boundaries

Being overwhelmed by too many responsibilities often leads to stress. Learning to manage your time and set boundaries can significantly reduce anxiety.

Here's how to do it:

Prioritize tasks: Focus on what's most important and tackle one thing at a time. Avoid trying to do everything at once.

Set realistic goals: Break complex tasks into smaller, achievable steps. Celebrate progress along the way.

Learn to say no: If you're stretched too thin, it's okay to decline additional responsibilities. Setting boundaries protects your mental and emotional well-being.

Breathing and Grounding Techniques

In moments of intense anxiety, breathing and grounding exercises can help you regain a sense of control. Besides controlled breathing, grounding techniques can also be effective in calming the mind.

One grounding technique is the 5-4-3-2-1 exercise:

Name five things you can see around you.

Name four things you can touch.

Name three things you can hear.

Name two things you can smell.

Name one thing you can taste.

This technique brings you back to the present, easing feelings of panic or overwhelm.

Long-Term Stress Reduction Strategies

In addition to short-term techniques, there are long-term habits you can develop to lower your overall stress levels:

Healthy eating: A balanced diet supports both physical and mental health. Avoid excessive caffeine, sugar, and processed foods, which can increase stress and anxiety.

Adequate sleep: Sleep is critical for mental resilience. Aim for seven to nine hours of quality sleep each night. If you struggle with sleep, establish a nightly routine that includes relaxation activities like reading, meditation, or gentle stretching.

Social connections: Strong relationships with friends, family, and your community are one of the best buffers against stress.

Community Support: The Power of Building Relationships

No one should face a crisis alone. Building relationships with your neighbors and local community provides critical support during difficult times. While self-reliance is important, having a network of people you can rely on can make all the difference when you feel overwhelmed or uncertain.

Why Community Support Matters

In times of crisis, communities that come together fare better than those where individuals are isolated. Your neighbors can offer physical, emotional, and practical support, whether through sharing resources, offering advice, or simply being there to listen. A strong community is also better equipped to coordinate responses to larger-scale emergencies, ensuring that everyone's needs are met.

How to Build Community Support

Building community support doesn't have to be complicated. Here are a few simple ways to start forming connections:

Get to Know Your Neighbors Introduce yourself to the people around you. Small interactions—like a friendly wave or offering help with a task—lay the foundation for stronger relationships. Knowing your neighbors makes it easier to reach out during a crisis when you already have an established connection.

Participate in Local Events Attend local gatherings like block parties, town meetings, or neighborhood watch groups. These events allow you to meet others in your area and strengthen community ties.

Share Resources and Skills One of the benefits of community is the ability to pool resources and expertise.

If you have a skill that could benefit others—such as gardening, carpentry, or first aid training—offer to share your knowledge. Likewise, don't hesitate to ask for help when you need it. A community where people freely share their resources is one that's better prepared for emergencies.

Form a Support Network Create a list of people in your community who you can turn to in times of need. Exchange contact information and discuss how you can help each other during a crisis. Whether it's offering a place to stay during a power outage or sharing food supplies, knowing who you can count on creates a sense of security.

Join Online Forums or Groups If you're unable to connect with people in person, online forums or neighborhood social media groups can be a great way to build a sense of community. Many local areas have Facebook groups or Next-door communities where residents can share information and offer help. These virtual spaces can be especially helpful for staying connected during lockdowns or other situations that limit physical interaction.

Strength in Unity

Emotional strength, stress management, and community support are crucial components of crisis preparedness. While it's important to stockpile physical resources and develop practical skills, the ability to stay calm, think clearly, and rely on others can make all the difference in how you navigate difficult times.

CHAPTER EIGHT

Real-Life Scenarios and Case Studies

When planning a bug-in strategy for survival, learning from historical crises and expert advice can be incredibly beneficial. The key is to understand what worked, what didn't, and how those lessons can be applied to your own situation. Whether you're staying put during a natural disaster, social unrest, or a pandemic, studying how others successfully navigated similar challenges can provide a blueprint for your survival.

Lessons from History: Successful Bug-In Strategies from Past Crises

History provides many examples of people sheltering in place during extended crises. From wartime blockades to pandemics, these situations offer valuable insights into how bug-in strategies can be effectively implemented.

The Siege of Sarajevo (1992-1996) During the Bosnian War, the Siege of Sarajevo lasted nearly four years. Residents had to survive under constant threat, with limited access to food, water, and electricity. They became resourceful, reusing materials for shelter, rationing food, and setting up makeshift water and electricity systems.

Key Takeaways:

Rationing: Carefully managing supplies helped civilians survive longer. This highlights the importance of stockpiling non-perishable food and learning to stretch supplies.

Water Access: Collecting rainwater and using nearby rivers became essential. A plan for water collection and purification is critical.

Community Support: Neighbors pooled resources and skills to help each other survive. The value of cooperation during a crisis cannot be overstated.

London Blitz (1940-1941) During World War II, Londoners sheltered in their homes or communal air raid shelters while enduring heavy bombing by Nazi Germany. Despite the dangers, they demonstrated incredible resilience.

Key Takeaways:

Mental Resilience: Psychological strength was crucial for surviving the Blitz. Maintaining routines, staying connected with family, and participating in community activities helped people cope.

Shelter: Reinforcing homes and using underground shelters saved lives. Fortifying your home to withstand threats is key in a bug-in scenario.

Stockpiling Essentials: Londoners stored essential goods, knowing resupply would be uncertain. Preparing with a stockpile of food, water, and medical supplies is vital.

COVID-19 Pandemic (2020) The COVID-19 pandemic is a recent example of a large-scale bug-in scenario, with people forced to stay home for months due to government-imposed lockdowns.

Key Takeaways:

Home Preparation: Those who had stocked up on essential supplies faced fewer challenges. Having a month's worth of food, sanitation products, and medical supplies is a wise precaution.

Mental Health: Prolonged isolation took a toll on mental health. Staying connected through technology, engaging in hobbies, and exercising helped many people cope.

Economic Stability: The importance of emergency savings became evident as job losses and income disruptions affected many. Having financial reserves is crucial.

Expert Insights: Practical Tips from Survival and Crisis Experts

Expert advice offers further guidance on how to prepare for and endure a bug-in situation.

Former Special Forces Soldier A retired Special Forces soldier shared his perspective on urban and rural survival strategies during a bug-in.

Key Takeaways:

Prioritize Security: Reinforcing doors and windows, setting up basic surveillance, and staying alert to potential threats are essential.

Situational Awareness: Keeping a low profile is critical. Stay indoors, minimize light and noise, and avoid attracting attention.

Redundancy: Have backup options for heating, lighting, and cooking. Whether it's a generator, solar panels, or a wood stove, multiple solutions increase your chances of survival.

Wilderness Survival Expert A seasoned survivalist shared tips that apply to both wilderness and home bug-in scenarios.

Key Takeaways:

Fire and Warmth: Staying warm is crucial. Learn how to start a fire indoors using a wood stove or fireplace.

Water Purification: Stockpiling water isn't enough. You need methods to purify water, whether through tablets, filters, or DIY filtration systems.

Psychological Resilience: A positive mindset is key to survival. Focusing on small victories, like making a meal or purifying water, keeps your mind sharp.

Emergency Preparedness Expert An expert in crisis management emphasized having a comprehensive bug-in plan.

Key Takeaways:

Communication Plans: Have backup communication methods like radios or satellite phones, and establish check-in times with family and friends.

Medical Supplies: Ensure you have prescription medications and know how to treat common injuries. First aid and CPR training are valuable.

Adaptability: Be ready to adjust your plans as situations change. Flexibility and quick thinking are crucial to survival.

Practical Applications: How to Implement These Strategies

Stockpiling Supplies:

Focus on non-perishable foods like canned goods, rice, and freeze-dried items. Rotate your stockpile to prevent expiration.

Store at least one gallon of water per person per day and invest in water purification methods.

Ensure you have hygiene supplies like toiletries and cleaning products.

Securing Your Shelter:

Fortify doors and windows with strong locks and metal reinforcements.

Prepare for power outages with multiple light sources like solar lanterns and battery-powered flashlights.

Health and Medical Preparedness:

Keep a well-stocked first aid kit and prescription medications.

Learn basic medical skills, like wound care and CPR.

Staying Informed:

Sign up for local emergency alerts.

Have a battery-powered radio to stay updated during power outages.

Mental Health Maintenance:

Establish a daily routine that includes exercise, meals, and leisure time.

Engage in activities that keep you mentally occupied, like reading or hobbies.

By taking these lessons and expert advice to heart, you'll be better prepared to handle any crisis that requires you to bug in, whether it's a natural disaster, pandemic, or civil unrest. Being ready ensures the safety and well-being of you and your loved ones.

CHAPTER NINE

Advanced Survival Skills

In any survival situation, especially when you choose to stay in place, having advanced skills can be the key difference between mere survival and truly thriving. Mastering areas such as home defense, food preservation, and emergency repairs will significantly increase your chances of staying safe and well-prepared. This chapter focuses on practical, hands-on skills for securing your home, preserving food for the long term, and maintaining essential systems during a disaster.

DIY Home Defense Projects

When you decide to shelter at home, securing your space becomes a top priority. During a crisis, relying on traditional law enforcement might not be possible, so it's important to take matters into your own hands.

Simple DIY projects can offer crucial layers of protection, safeguarding your home, loved ones, and resources.

Creating Noise Alarms A basic noise alarm system can alert you to intruders before they reach your home. While advanced alarm systems are ideal, they may fail in power outages or long-term emergencies. Fortunately, you can create effective noise alarms with simple materials.

What You'll Need:

Empty cans or bottles

String or fishing line

Bells or metal scraps

Nails or hooks

How It Works: Tie the string or fishing line around cans or metal pieces and hang them along potential entry points, such as windows or fences. When someone disturbs the string, the cans or bells will rattle, creating noise and alerting you to their presence. These low-tech alarms are affordable, don't rely on electricity, and provide an early warning system during extended crises.

Reinforcing Windows and Doors Windows and doors are your home's most vulnerable entry points. While installing deadbolts and sturdy locks is a good start, there are additional DIY projects that can make these areas more secure.

What You'll Need:

Wooden dowels or metal rods

Plywood or metal sheets

Reinforcement brackets

Shatter-resistant window film

How It Works: For windows, cut dowels or rods to fit snugly in the track of sliding windows or doors, preventing them from being forced open. Applying shatter-resistant film adds further protection by making windows harder to break. For doors, reinforce the frame with metal plates or brackets, especially where the deadbolt meets the doorframe. In extreme situations, consider boarding up windows with plywood or metal sheets for added security.

Building Simple Traps In worst-case scenarios, where law enforcement is no longer operational, setting traps around your property may become necessary to deter or slow intruders. Always ensure these traps are safe for your family, pets, and innocent visitors.

What You'll Need:

Nails or spikes

Rope or fishing line

Boards or plywood

Heavy objects (bricks, metal bars)

How It Works: A basic trap involves embedding nails or spikes into a board, then burying it just below the surface near access points. This trap should only be used in extreme cases, with clear warnings to avoid harming unintended targets. You can also create tripwire traps by attaching heavy objects to fishing lines that drop when triggered, slowing down intruders.

Food Preservation Techniques

In a disaster, food security is as critical as physical safety. Without refrigeration or regular access to grocery stores, knowing how to preserve food for months or even years is essential. Several simple methods can extend food shelf life and are manageable with basic household equipment.

Canning Canning is one of the most reliable methods for long-term food preservation, allowing you to store items for years.

What You'll Need:

Mason jars with lids

A large pot or pressure canner

Tongs

Fresh produce or meat

How It Works: For high-acid foods like fruit and tomatoes, use water bath canning by boiling the filled jars for the appropriate amount of time. Low-acid foods like meat and vegetables require a pressure canner to kill harmful bacteria. Store sealed jars in a cool, dark place and label them with contents and dates.

Dehydrating Dehydrating removes moisture from food, preventing bacterial growth and allowing it to last for extended periods.

What You'll Need:

A dehydrator or oven

Baking sheets or dehydrator trays

Fresh produce or meat

How It Works: Slice food into thin, even pieces, spread them on trays, and dry them in a dehydrator or oven at a low temperature. Store dried items in airtight containers or vacuum-sealed bags. Dehydrated food can be rehydrated by adding water, making it perfect for soups and stews in a survival situation.

Pickling Pickling preserves food by soaking it in a vinegar, salt, and spice solution, which creates an acidic environment that inhibits bacteria growth.

What You'll Need:

Fresh vegetables or fruit

Vinegar, salt, and optional spices

Jars with lids

How It Works: Prepare your vegetables, mix the pickling solution, and pour it over the produce in jars. Seal and store the jars in a cool, dark place. Pickled foods add flavor and variety to your diet during long-term survival situations.

Fermentation - Fermentation uses beneficial bacteria to preserve food and is ideal for making items like sauerkraut and kimchi, which also boost gut health.

What You'll Need:

Fresh vegetables (e.g., cabbage for sauerkraut)

Salt

A large jar or crock

How It Works: Shred vegetables, mix with salt, and pack tightly into a jar. The salt draws moisture out, creating a brine where fermentation takes place. Fermented foods can last for months and provide nutritional benefits.

Emergency Repairs and Maintenance

During an extended crisis, professional repairs might not be available, making DIY repairs crucial to maintaining your home's safety and functionality.

Basic Plumbing Repairs Issues like burst pipes or clogged drains can quickly make your home uninhabitable if not addressed.

What You'll Need:

Pipe wrench

Plumber's tape

PVC pipe and fittings

Plunger or drain snake

How It Works: If a pipe bursts, shut off the water and replace the damaged section with new pipe, using plumber's tape to seal the joints. For clogged drains, use a plunger or snake to remove blockages.

Roof Repairs A leaky roof can lead to severe damage if left untreated.

What You'll Need:

Roofing nails

Roofing tar

Replacement shingles or metal sheeting

Ladder, hammer

How It Works: Find the source of the leak, apply roofing tar, and replace damaged shingles. For more severe damage, patch larger sections to prevent further issues.

Electrical Repairs Basic electrical knowledge can help you handle minor issues like blown fuses or faulty switches.

What You'll Need:

Voltage tester

Wire cutters

Electrical tape

Replacement fuses or breakers

How It Works: If a fuse blows or a breaker trips, replace or reset them. For minor repairs, ensure the power is off before working on wiring, and always use electrical tape to insulate exposed wires.

Patching Walls and Floors Wear and tear can cause cracks and holes in walls and floors, leading to more significant problems.

What You'll Need:

Spackle or joint compound

Sandpaper

Drywall patches

Paint, nails, or screws

How It Works: Use spackle or joint compound to fill small holes in drywall, or replace damaged sections with patches. For floors, fill cracks with wood filler or grout, depending on the material.

These advanced survival skills—home defense, food preservation, and emergency repairs—are essential for maintaining a secure and functional household during a crisis. By mastering these techniques, you'll be well-equipped to protect yourself, your family, and your property, no matter how long the emergency lasts. Preparing now ensures you're ready for whatever comes your way.

CHAPTER 10

Reclaiming Joy and Living with Peace

When facing a crisis at home, having a solid plan can be the difference between chaos and calm. A bug-in strategy is essential if you've determined that staying put is the safest and most practical choice during a disaster. Whether it's a natural disaster, civil unrest, or an extended power outage, a well-prepared plan will help you stay organized and ready for anything.

This chapter walks you through creating a customized bug-in plan. We'll cover everything from what to do before a crisis hits, the crucial supplies you'll need, and the steps to secure your home and protect your family. We'll also discuss the importance of regularly updating your plan based on what you learn along the way.

Step-by-Step Guide: How to Create a Personalized Bug-In Plan

1. Assess Your Situation

Start by understanding your unique circumstances, as no two households are the same. Tailor your bug-in plan to your specific needs by asking essential questions:

Who will be with you? Consider the number of people in your household and their individual needs, including children, elderly family members, or pets. Account for any medical conditions or other requirements that need extra planning.

What risks are most likely in your area? Depending on where you live, certain hazards may be more likely. For example, coastal residents should prepare for hurricanes, while those in earthquake-prone areas should focus on structural safety. If civil unrest is a concern, home security becomes a top priority.

What is your home's layout? Understanding your home's vulnerabilities, such as entry points like doors and windows, is key to reinforcing them. Also, plan where to store emergency supplies for easy access during a crisis.

2. Stockpile Essential Supplies

After assessing your situation, gather the supplies you'll need to survive a disaster at home. Aim for at least a two-week supply of food, water, medical necessities, and other essentials—but planning for a month or more is even better.

Food and Water:

Water: Store a minimum of one gallon per person per day for drinking, cooking, and hygiene. A two-week supply means 14 gallons per person. Don't forget about pets' water needs, and consider water purification tablets or a filtration system in case your supply becomes contaminated.

Food: Focus on non-perishable items like canned goods, rice, pasta, and freeze-dried meals. Include kitchen staples like salt and spices. If you have babies or family members with dietary restrictions, stock up on appropriate foods and formula.

Medical Supplies:

First Aid Kit: Keep a well-stocked kit with bandages, antiseptics, pain relievers, and any necessary prescription medications. If trained, include items for more serious injuries like tourniquets or sutures.

Hygiene Products: Stock items like soap, hand sanitizer, toothpaste, and feminine hygiene supplies. Consider no-rinse wipes and dry shampoo if water is limited.

3. Secure Your Home

Your home becomes your sanctuary in a crisis, so it's essential to make it as secure as possible. Focus on reinforcing vulnerable entry points and protecting against intruders or storm damage.

Reinforce Entry Points:

Doors: Install heavy-duty deadbolts and reinforce frames with metal plates. Replace any hollow-core doors with solid wood or metal options for better security.

Windows: Use shatter-resistant film to strengthen windows and add dowels to sliding doors and windows to prevent them from being forced open.

Garage Doors: Ensure your garage is securely locked, and if it's electric, know how to operate it manually in case of a power outage.

Install a Security System: Even a basic system with backup power or motion-activated lights can deter intruders. For long-term crises, consider adding noise alarms or simple traps for extra protection.

4. Plan for Power Outages

Power outages are common in many crisis situations. Plan ahead to stay warm, cook, and charge essential electronics.

Backup Power:

Generators: A generator can be a lifesaver during extended power outages. Ensure you have enough fuel to last several days. Solar-powered generators are an alternative, though they can be more expensive.

Battery Backup: For smaller needs, like charging phones or powering small devices, a battery backup or power bank is crucial.

Heating and Cooling:

Heating: If you live in a cold climate, stockpile blankets, sleeping bags, and firewood if you have a fireplace. Portable propane heaters can also help, but ensure proper ventilation to avoid carbon monoxide poisoning.

Cooling: In warmer areas, battery-powered fans or solar-powered cooling devices are essential. Stay hydrated to avoid heat-related illnesses.

5. Establish an Emergency Communication Plan

Communication is vital in a crisis, especially if you need to check on loved ones or coordinate with neighbors.

Family Communication Plan:

Designate a Meeting Place: Choose an indoor and outdoor meeting spot in case it's unsafe to stay inside.

Check-ins: Set regular check-in times to ensure everyone is safe. Routine can help reduce panic.

Alternative Communication Methods:

Walkie-talkies: These are great for short-range communication, especially if cell service is down.

Ham Radio: For large-scale disasters, a ham radio is one of the most reliable communication tools, though it requires training.

Checklists for Preparedness: Essential Items and Tasks

Creating a comprehensive checklist ensures you don't overlook anything important. Here are some key areas to cover:

Food and Water Checklist:

14+ gallons of water per person

Water purification tablets or filters

Non-perishable food for at least two weeks

Alternative cooking methods and fuel

Medical and Hygiene Checklist:

Fully stocked first aid kit

Prescription medications

Over-the-counter medicine (pain relievers, cold medicine)

Hygiene products

Tools and Equipment Checklist:

Flashlights, lanterns, and extra batteries

Multi-tool and basic hand tools

Fire extinguisher

Matches or lighters

Security Checklist:

Reinforce doors and windows

Install motion-sensor lights or security cameras

Secure garage doors

Power and Heating Checklist:

Generator with sufficient fuel or solar-powered alternative

Battery backup for small devices

Blankets, warm clothes, or cooling equipment

Communication Checklist:

Family communication plan
Walkie-talkies

Battery-powered radio or ham radio

Review and Adaptation: Keep Your Plan Updated

Your bug-in plan should evolve as your circumstances change. Here's how to ensure it stays relevant:

Learn from Past Experiences: After every crisis, assess what worked and what didn't. Use these lessons to improve your plan.

Stay Informed: Keep up with local news and emergency alerts to stay aware of new risks in your area.

Practice Regularly: Conduct family drills to make sure everyone knows what to do and how to use essential equipment.

Final Thoughts

Creating a personalized bug-in plan is about more than just survival—it's about thriving in uncertain times. By preparing carefully and staying proactive, you can ensure your family's safety and peace of mind, no matter what challenges arise.

CONCLUSION

Empower Your Home Defense

When it comes to protecting your home and loved ones, preparedness is your strongest defense. The Navy SEALs Bug-In Guide has equipped you with the knowledge and mindset to turn your home into a fortress capable of withstanding any threat. But remember, knowledge without action is just theory. The time to act is now—before danger arrives at your doorstep.

Be Prepared Before the Crisis

A solid defense starts with preparation. Whether facing natural disasters, civil unrest, or other dangers, you now have step-by-step guidance to identify and strengthen your home's vulnerabilities. Securing entry points, building a reliable stockpile, and developing a family emergency plan are not optional—they are essential. Take these steps now so that when the unexpected strikes, you remain calm, collected, and ready.

Adapt and Overcome

A key lesson from this guide is the importance of adaptability. Crises rarely unfold as expected, and you may encounter unforeseen challenges. But with the Navy SEAL mindset of improvising, adapting, and overcoming, you can approach any situation with confidence. Stay open to learning and refining your plans as you move forward. The more flexible you are, the more resilient you'll become.

Protect What Matters Most

At the heart of this guide is the mission to safeguard what matters most: your family, your home, and your peace of mind. The confidence that comes from knowing you're prepared to face any danger is invaluable. Your home is your sanctuary, and with the strategies outlined in this guide, you now have the blueprint to secure it against whatever may come.

Take action today—make the safety of your home a top priority. Preparedness isn't about fear—it's about empowerment.

Made in United States
Troutdale, OR
12/20/2024

27013331R00082